21st Century Junior Library

DISCOVER THE MAMMOTH

Jennifer Zeiger

Our Prehistoric World: Beyond Dinosaurs

Published in the United States of America by:

CHERRY LAKE PRESS
2395 South Huron Parkway, Suite 200, Ann Arbor, Michigan 48104
www.cherrylakepress.com

Content Adviser: Gregory M. Erickson, PhD, Dinosaur Paleontologist, Department of Biological Science, Florida State University, Tallahassee, Florida

Reading Adviser: Beth Walker Gambro, MS, Ed., Reading Consultant, Yorkville, IL

Photo and Illustration Credits: © Warpaint/Shutterstock, cover, title page; © Orla/iStock.com, 5; © Daniel Eskridge/Shutterstock, 6; © Esteban De Armas/Shutterstock, 7; © Dotted Yeti/Shutterstock, 8–9; © Aunt Spray/Shutterstock, 10; © Daniel Eskridge/Shutterstock, 11; © Dotted Yeti/Shutterstock, 12–13; © Aunt Spray/Shutterstock, 14; © buradaki/iStock.com, 16 (inset); Dantheman9758 at the English Wikipedia, CC BY-SA 3.0 via Wikimedia Commons, 17; Jllm06, CC BY-SA 4.0 via Wikimedia Commons, 18–19; © New Africa/Shutterstock, 19; Cave painter, Public domain, via Wikimedia Commons, 20

Cherry Lake Press is an imprint of Cherry Lake Publishing Group.

Library of Congress Cataloging-in-Publication Data has been filed and is available at catalog.loc.gov.

Cherry Lake Press would like to acknowledge the work of the Partnership for 21st Century Learning, a Network of Battelle for Kids. Please visit Battelle for Kids online for more information.

Printed in the United States of America

Note from publisher: Websites change regularly, and their future contents are outside of our control. Supervise children when conducting any recommended online searches for extended learning opportunities.

CHERRY LAKE PRESS

CONTENTS

WHAT WAS A MAMMOTH?

Picture a group of **prehistoric** elephants. They are covered in hair. The hair may be long and woolly. The animals munch on grass in a wide field. These are mammoths. This ancient animal was related to the elephants we know today.

Mammoths lived in family groups called **herds**. The males left the herds when they grew up.

The word *mammoth* can be used to describe something big. And these animals were really big! In fact, mammoths were named for being so large. Most mammoths were about the size of today's elephants. Some were much bigger!

Woolly mammoths could weigh from 12,000 to 16,000 pounds (5443.1 to 7257.5 kilograms).

Make a Guess!

We know that humans met mammoths. But how do we know? Make a guess. Then read on to find out if you were right!

Mammoths first appeared about 5 million years ago. They lived for millions of years. Early humans even hunted them for a time. There are no mammoths living today, though. They are **extinct**.

WHAT DID A MAMMOTH LOOK LIKE?

Mammoths looked a lot like elephants. They had large heads and wide, flat ears. They also had very long noses called trunks. Two big teeth called tusks stuck out of their mouths. Mammoth tusks often curled up towards the face. These animals had large, heavy bodies. Four thick, strong legs supported them. They also had tall, dome-shaped skulls like elephants.

The largest mammoth tusks ever found were over 16 feet (4.9 meters) long.

Elephants today do not have much hair. The Columbian mammoth likely didn't either. The Columbian mammoth lived in North America. It was the largest mammoth. Scientists have found preserved mammoth hair. The hair ranged from yellowish brown to reddish brown.

Create!

Mammoths were very similar to other prehistoric animals called mastodons. Look up pictures of both in books or online with an adult. Now draw your own mammoth and mastodon. Label the ways they are different from each other.

The climate in North America at the time was temperate. The Columbian mammoth didn't need thick fur.

Northern mammoths had the thickest hair. One type of mammoth was called the woolly mammoth for its long, thick hair.

Think!

We know a lot about woolly mammoths. Scientists have been able to study their well-preserved remains. What do you think helped preserve them?

Baby mammoths stayed close to their moms.

HOW DID A MAMMOTH LIVE?

Mammoths lived across North America and Central America. They were also found in Asia, Europe, and Africa. Mammoths usually lived in open **grasslands**. That's because they mostly ate grass. This food was easy to find in grasslands.

Mammoths had wide, **ridged** teeth. These ground up the food the mammoth chewed.

Ask Questions!

What questions do you have about how teeth help scientists learn about animals? Make a plan to find answers.

When woolly mammoths lived, global temperatures were 11 degrees Fahrenheit (6 degrees Celsius) cooler. Glaciers covered half of North and South America, Europe, and much of Asia.

The Mammoth Site in Hot Springs, South Dakota was once a prehistoric sinkhole. It holds at least 61 mammoth skeletons.

The bones of many mammoths are often found together. This leads experts to believe that mammoths lived in herds. This is also how elephants live today.

Rouffignac Cave in France is known as the "Cave of the Hundred Mammoths." There are prehistoric paintings on the walls of mammoths, rhinos, horses, and bison.

We learn about mammoths in many ways. One way is from **fossils**. People have also found whole bodies frozen in ice. These animals even appear in cave paintings. People drew these pictures thousands of years ago. But we still do not know everything. There is always more to learn about these ancient animals!

Look!

Look up some pictures of cave paintings. Ask an adult to help you find the best ones. What shapes, animals, and other objects are in the paintings? Do you see anything surprising?

GLOSSARY

extinct **(ik-STINKT)** no longer found anywhere on Earth

fossils **(FAH-suhlz)** remains or traces of plants, animals, and other living things that have been preserved as rocks

glaciers **(GLAY-shuhrz)** large bodies of ice that move slowly over land

grasslands **(GRAS-landz)** large, open areas of grass

herds **(HURDZ)** large groups of animals that stay or move together

prehistoric **(pree-hih-STOR-ik)** belonging to a time before history was recorded in written form

ridged **(RIJD)** having narrow, raised strips on the surface

sinkhole **(SINK-hohl)** hole or depression in the ground caused by a collapse of the surface

FIND OUT MORE

Books

Lopetz, Christian. *Rise of the Giant Mammals.* Ann Arbor, MI: Cherry Lake Publishing, 2026.

Murray, Julie. *Woolly Mammoth.* Minneapolis, MN: ABDO, 2023.

Tite, Jack. *Mega Meltdown: The Weird and Wonderful Animals of the Ice Age.* New York, NY: Blueprint Editions, 2018.

Websites

With an adult, learn more online with these suggested searches.

American Museum of Natural History: Mammoth or Mastodon?
Learn how to tell the difference between these prehistoric animals.

PBS Learning Media: Mammoths | Science Trek
Explore what scientists have learned about mammoths and how they lived.

INDEX

ABOUT THE AUTHOR

Jennifer Zeiger lives in Chicago, Illinois. She writes and edits children's books on all sorts of topics.

ABOUT PALEOARTISTS

Paleoartists bring the prehistoric world to life! They work with scientists, paleontologists, museums, and their own research to recreate living things from long, long ago. **Mark Witton** is one paleoartist featured in this series. He has been studying prehistoric creatures for over 20 years! **Brian Engh** is another. He builds sculptures, too. He designs and builds whole exhibits. He started Living Relic Productions.